Mandala Wonder

Swear Word

Almond Vinnie

Mandala Wonder

Swear Word

Copyright: Published in the United States **by Almond Vinnie**
Published August 2016

ISBN-13: 978-1537073170
ISBN-10: 1537073176

Swear
Word

Bullshit

Piss Off

Asshole

Bitch

Fuck

SLUT

Bastard

where

Douche

Fuckwit

Twat
Waffle

Wanker

Cum
Guzzler

Beaver
Dam

cupcake

slutbag

Asshat

Moron

Fuck Off

Skank

Cockbag

Dickhead

June

Baggy
Vag

fucktard

Prick

Cunt Muffin

Dipshit

THANK YOU

www.ingramcontent.com/pod-product-compliance
Lightning Source LLC
Chambersburg PA
CBHW080324290526
45793CB00006B/1205
9781537073170